# GENETICALLY MODIFIED
# FOODS

*Essential Viewpoints*

# GENETICALLY MODIFIED

# FOODS

BY LILLIAN E. FORMAN

**Content Consultant**
Stephen Nottingham, PhD
Science Writer and Consultant

**ABDO**
Publishing Company

# CREDITS

Published by ABDO Publishing Company, 8000 West 78th Street, Edina, Minnesota 55439. Copyright © 2010 by Abdo Consulting Group, Inc. International copyrights reserved in all countries. No part of this book may be reproduced in any form without written permission from the publisher. The Essential Library™ is a trademark and logo of ABDO Publishing Company.

Printed in the United States.

Editor: Rebecca Rowell
Copy Editor: Paula Lewis
Interior Design and Production: Nicole Brecke
Cover Design: Nicole Brecke

**Library of Congress Cataloging-in-Publication Data**
Forman, Lillian E.
  Genetically modified foods / by Lillian E. Forman.
      p. cm. — (Essential viewpoints)
  Includes bibliographical references and index.
  ISBN 978-1-60453-531-0
  1.  Genetically modified foods—Juvenile literature.  I. Title.
  TP248.65.F66F74 2009
  641.3—dc22

                          2008034906

# TABLE OF CONTENTS

James Watson and Francis Crick, photographed in 1959,
discovered DNA's structure.

# BREAKTHROUGHS
# IN BIOLOGY

In 1953, James Watson and Francis Crick
published an exciting paper in the science
journal *Nature*. It opened a door to possibilities
that had been considered in the realm of science
fiction. Their paper described the structure of

deoxyribonucleic acid (DNA), a molecule containing the units of heredity. Watson and Crick demonstrated that the DNA molecule takes the form of a double helix, which resembles a ladder that has been twisted into a spiral.

Genes are the building blocks of DNA. The discovery of DNA's structure made it possible for biologists to understand how genes direct the synthesis of protein. Genes interact with the environment to determine the characteristics of every living organism—its appearance, development, and behavior. Genes are passed from parent to offspring. By isolating and manipulating genes, scientists have the power to transform and create living organisms. Watson and Crick's discovery has led to a new scientific field called genetic engineering.

**DNA**

The structure of the DNA molecule is important to understanding how genes operate. Hereditary information is programmed in the DNA through the arrangements of the chemical base pairs. These pairs form the rungs of the ladderlike double helix. The sequence of base pairs is called the genetic code. A gene is a functional unit of this code. The complete information held in an organism's DNA is its genome.

## GENETIC ENGINEERING ACHIEVEMENTS

In 1973, researchers transferred DNA from a virus into a bacterium. Scientists then made human insulin for treating diabetes from genetically

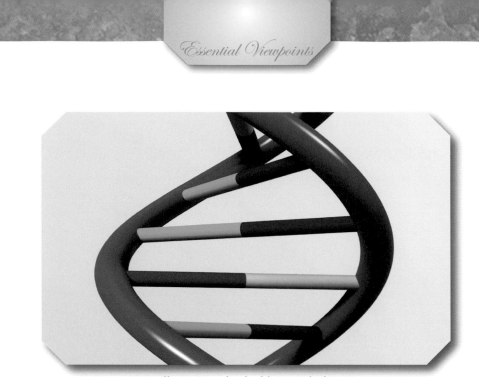

An illustration of a double strand of DNA

modified bacteria, a process that was patented
in 1980.

Agribusinesses are companies that manufacture
and sell crop seed, pesticides, farm equipment,
and supplies. Agribusiness leaders realized that this
new technology could help them increase profits.
They hired genetic engineers to design crop plants
with desirable traits. These plants became known
as genetically modified, genetically engineered, or
transgenic plants. Here, the term *genetically modified*
refers to organisms that have been modified through
the science of genetic engineering.

The first generation of genetically modified crop plants could tolerate large doses of weed killers, produce their own insecticide to resist harmful insects, and stay at peak ripeness for unusually long periods. When accused by consumer groups of using biotechnology solely for their own gains, food industrialists argued that the genetic engineering of food could bring about social and commercial benefits. They pointed to the "golden rice" developed by scientists Peter Beyer and Ingo Potrykus in 1999. This rice will be freely available to plant-breeding centers in the developing world. It has been modified to produce the chemical beta-carotene that is not in ordinary rice.

Beta-carotene enables animals to manufacture vitamin A, which is essential for good health. Rice lacks vitamin A. Many Asian children eat mostly rice, so they do not get enough vitamin A. Worldwide, approximately 1 million children die from diseases caused by weak immune systems, and 350,000 preschool-age children become blind. The beta-carotene provided in the golden rice would increase the amount of vitamin A in the children's diets. This could help decrease the number of deaths and cases of blindness.

Genetic engineers are working on a range of projects that will have social benefits similar to golden rice. For example, scientists are developing fruits and vegetables that contain vaccines against certain diseases. Also in development are plants that can filter harmful substances from the soil as well as those that can thrive under drought conditions.

## OBJECTIONS TO GENETICALLY MODIFIED FOOD

Several groups oppose genetically modified foods. Many of their fears stem from the fact that genetic engineering is a relatively young science. Opponents believe the risks of genetically modified food were not adequately assessed before the food was introduced to consumers.

Nathan B. Batalion is a strong critic of genetically modified foods. In his article "50 Harmful Effects of Genetically Modified Foods," he warns these foods can kill. Batalion cites a study in which a gene from a Brazil nut plant was introduced to a soybean plant to nutritionally enhance the soybean food crop. People known to be allergic to Brazil nuts experienced allergic reactions when they ate the modified soybeans. Allergens can prove fatal for some people. The worry is that not all genetically modified food will be tested thoroughly prior to marketing.

Batalion also fears that food containing genes from other sources might cause cancer. He notes action taken by the U.S. Food and Drug Administration (FDA) in 1994. Batalion claims the FDA approved injection of cows with a genetically modified growth hormone called rBGH despite a study that suggested doing so might increase the risk for disease in humans.

In addition, Batalion and other critics warn against an increase in human resistance to antibiotics. Genes that produce antibiotics are included in genetically modified plants along with other foreign genes. This is done so antibiotic treatments can be used to select plants that have successfully taken up the foreign genes. These plants are often used in animal feed. When people consume the meat and milk of animals fed these plants, their digestive system breaks down the DNA of the genetically modified foods. Bacteria in a person's digestive system might absorb genes for

## Using Enzymes

An enzyme is a protein that acts as a catalyst, or promoter, for a particular chemical reaction. The cells of plants and animals use a wide range of enzymes to promote the chemical reactions that help organisms carry out life functions. One set of enzymes is dedicated to maintaining and replicating DNA. Genetic engineers use versions of these enzymes to precisely cut out sections of DNA, paste these sections into new genomes, and duplicate them.

antibiotic resistance. This may add to the increasing tolerance for antibiotics among humans, which makes fighting infections with antibiotics more difficult.

Batalion also stresses that food created from genetically modified crops will be less nutritious than food created from conventional crops. He and other consumer advocates believe marketing genetically modified food without identifying it as such shows a greater concern for profit than for the public.

Critics also have many ecological concerns related to genetically

## Manipulating Nature Is Not New

More than 10,000 years ago, farmers influenced the evolution of plants and animals by selectively breeding species with traits that best suited their needs.

Biotechnology began with using yeasts to ferment fruits and grains to make liquors and bread. These and subsequent means of processing food affected the selection of plants and animals. Those reacting most favorably to the new processes were selected for cultivation.

In the mid-1800s, Gregor Mendel, an Austrian monk, made selective breeding a science. He found that some traits are dominant and others are recessive. His discovery gave humans greater power over nature.

Mutations are sudden inheritable changes in genetic material that produce new traits. Biologist Hugo de Vries discovered mutations in the early 1900s. Farmers soon learned how to incorporate more desirable new traits into the gene pool of their plants and livestock.

The work of Mendel and de Vries was the foundation for modern genetics and selective breeding. Modern genetic engineers state that their technology is not unnatural but simply the next logical step in agricultural progress.

modified plants and animals. They fear these organisms will diminish the diversity and abundance of species as a result of crossbreeding.

## The Heart of the Controversy

Scientists point to the many benefits of genetically modified food. They claim the technology can program organisms to produce vaccines and medicinal drugs. Genetically modified food can have greater nutritional value than food created from conventional crops. It also can be used to produce plants that resist weed killers (herbicides) and plants that have a built-in resistance to insect pests. Finally, genetic engineers say they can develop plants and animals that need fewer resources to survive.

Opponents of genetically modified food highlight several concerns. They argue that genetic engineering of plants and animals for food and medicine is expensive and impractical. Genetically modified products are not labeled as such in the United States. This raises concern that U.S. consumers are not fully aware of what they are buying. These consumers cannot protect themselves against the perceived risks of such food. Consumers with allergies, vegetarians, and people who follow religious dietary rules cannot avoid food that might contain genes derived from forbidden organisms. Also, genetically modified plants may threaten plant diversity and ecological systems. If genetically modified crops are designed to withstand large amounts of herbicide, nearby crops or wild plants may be damaged by overspraying. Hybrids produced by the cross-pollination of genetically modified plants and plants free of genetic modification might outcompete other plants and change the species balance in natural habitats. Genetically modified plants with built-in resistance to harmful insects might kill beneficial insects. Some opponents believe genetic engineers should not interfere with natural processes. Others fear that acquiring patents for new genetically modified products is slowly enabling agribusinesses to dominate world food production.

It is unknown whether genetically modified organisms are a solution to problems such as hunger, disease, and poverty. People on both sides of the controversy present strong arguments for and against the new technology.

*Demonstrators carry signs expressing their concern over genetically modified food during a protest in Chicago, Illinois, in November 1999.*

*Organic produce is now available in many supermarkets.*

# ORGANIC FOOD

Humans have been selectively breeding food plants and animals for thousands of years. Before genetic engineering, some consumers felt that food from conventional crops grown with synthetic pesticides and insecticides was inferior to that grown organically, without synthetic chemicals. In 1962, Rachel Carson's book *Silent Spring* warned readers about the increasing use of chemical pesticides and herbicides, particularly DDT (dichloro-diphenyl-trichloroethane). The chemicals can harm animals and humans. Carson's book aroused such public outcry that the U.S. government banned the use of DDT in 1972.

Some people never regained faith in the various U.S. agencies entrusted to protect U.S. consumers from hazardous food, drugs, and environmental conditions. Many people began demanding stronger guarantees that food is truly safe and nutritious.

## ORGANIC FOODS PRODUCTION ACT

Methods of growing crops and processing food have not always been consistent among organic farmers and food processors. In 1990, the U.S. Congress passed the Organic Foods Production Act. This legislation required the U.S. Department of Agriculture to set certain standards for food before it can be certified as organic.

**Lab Rats on Organic Diets**

According to scientists at Newcastle University in the United Kingdom and the Danish Institute, rats fed organic foods are slimmer, sleep better, and have stronger immune systems than those fed conventionally grown produce.

According to the act, organic food must be grown without pesticides, artificial fertilizers, and genetically modified material. The act requires organic farmers and food processors to keep records of the fertilizers and other materials they use and their methods of storage, cleaning, and waste disposal. Before food products can be labeled as organic, they must contain 95 percent certified organic material. The other 5 percent must be natural substances that do not occur in organic form, such as minerals.

## Advantages of Organic Food

Groups of organic-food growers and advocates worldwide make many claims in favor of organic food based on experimental studies. They state that such food is safer, more nutritious, and better tasting than food made from crops treated with artificial chemicals or from genetically engineered plants. They also claim that organic food can prevent or alleviate illnesses.

In 2003, Allison Byrum of the American Chemical Society reported that organic vegetables and fruits contain more antioxidants than food that is genetically engineered or treated with chemicals.

Among other benefits, antioxidants fight cancer in humans. Plants produce antioxidants to protect themselves from insects. Byrum explained that the artificial pesticides used on conventionally grown crops make it unnecessary for crops to manufacture these natural defenses. Alternatively, the natural fertilizers used by organic farmers encourage the production of antioxidants.

The Organic Trade Association (OTA) represents the organic industry in Canada, Mexico, and the United States. In 2006, the OTA published a compilation of studies by various researchers worldwide. According to the OTA, a lot of organic food has more vitamin C, iron, magnesium, and phosphorus and fewer toxic ingredients than conventionally grown food. The various studies also indicated that organically grown plants are less likely to contain harmful strains of *E. coli* than other types of food. *E. coli* is a type of bacteria that can cause

**Organic Farming and Global Warming**

The Rodale Institute conducted a 15-year study titled "Farming Systems Trial." The study found that organic agriculture can reduce greenhouse gas emissions. Organic agriculture locks more carbon into the soil than it releases into the atmosphere, which is what happens in conventional agriculture. The study showed that using organic fertilizer in the major corn and soybean regions of the United States could reduce atmospheric carbon dioxide levels by an estimated 2 percent.

episodes of severe diarrhea, vomiting, and high fever.

Organic-food advocates argue that organic farming also helps the environment. In *The State of the World 1999*, Lester Brown and associates claim that synthetic pesticides can damage helpful organisms. The authors note,

> *In the United States, populations of honeybees, essential for pollinating commercial crops, have shrunk precipitously [quickly and sharply], while frogs with missing eyes and extra legs have been found in northern states. Pesticides are leading suspects behind both aberrations [abnormalities].[1]*

Other proponents of organic food argue that organic farming techniques, such as certain methods of crop rotation, help to maintain a healthy ecology. Furthermore, many synthetic pesticides are oil based and are becoming more expensive to produce.

## CHALLENGES TO ORGANIC FOOD

Despite the endorsements of organic food, some people doubt that it is less harmful and more nutritious than other food. Gregory E. Pence is a professor of bioethics in the Philosophy Department and School of Medicine at the University of Alabama at Birmingham. Pence asserts in *Designer Food: Mutant Harvest or Breadbasket of the World?* that organically grown food is not necessarily safer than genetically modified food. He argues that the natural manure used in organic farming is a breeding ground for *E. coli* and other bacteria. He cites two incidents as evidence. In 1996, unpasteurized apple juice infected with *E. coli* resulted in the death of one child in the Pacific Northwest and made 66 other people seriously ill. In 2000, organic mushrooms tested

**Crop Rotation**

Farmers rotate their crops to preserve soil fertility, prevent soil erosion, and control pests. George Kuepper and Lance Gegner are agricultural specialists at the National Center for Appropriate Technology (NCAT). They feel the basic Midwestern rotation is especially effective:

- *Legumes [plants such as peas or beans] fix nitrogen in the soil, providing for subsequent non-legumes in the rotation. [Nitrogen plays a vital role in plant development.]*
- *Several insect pest cycles are interrupted, especially those of . . . rootworm species that can be devastating to corn.*
- *Several plant diseases are suppressed, including soybean cyst nematode.*
- *Weed control is enhanced as perennial weeds [lasting for more than two growing seasons] are destroyed through cultivation of annual grains; most annual weeds [lasting one growing season] are smothered or eliminated by mowing when alfalfa is in production.*
- *Livestock manures (if available) are applied just in advance of corn, a heavy nitrogen consumer.*
- *All crops can be marketed either as is or fed to livestock to be converted into value-added milk, meat or other livestock products.*[2]

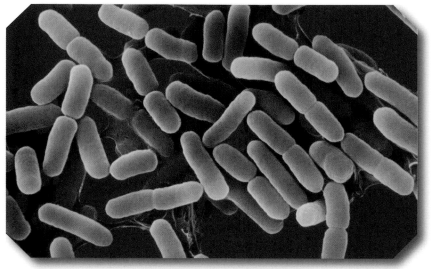

*A scanning electron image of* E. coli

positive for *E. coli* and had to be removed from supermarket shelves.

Organic farmers describe many of the pesticides they use as environmentally friendly because they are derived from natural sources rather than manufactured with chemicals. Pence declares that some of these natural pesticides are as deadly as any poison developed by humans. For example, rotenone is a substance extracted from the roots of certain tropical plants. In 2000, researchers at Emory University injected rats with rotenone. These rats tended to develop symptoms of a Parkinson's-like disease, an illness that results in the loss of control of normal body movements. As for danger presented by unknown allergens in genetically modified food, Pence assures people that genetically modified food is more thoroughly tested for such dangers than the exotic fruits and vegetables imported from developing countries.

In addition, Pence disputes the assertion that organic food is more nutritious than genetically modified food. He points out that transferred genes originate in nature and will produce the same benefits in the modified organism as those that appear naturally in organic food.

Pence challenges the claim that organic farming techniques are better for the environment than the techniques used on farms where genetically modified organisms are raised. He explains that acquiring enough manure for fertilizing organic crops involves destroying the environment. In response to the charge that genetically modified organisms might take over ecosystems and crowd out other organisms, Pence observes that farmers have altered the genetics of their crops and livestock for centuries. Farmers have grown plants or animals that best met their needs. As a result, the selected organisms have developed differently from early generations and sometimes replaced them.

Pence also notes the enormous amount of work needed to grow organic produce. Paying the laborers required to do such work increases the cost of organic food beyond the reach of a large part of the world's population. Also, more fuel is needed to grow organic food on a large scale. Farmers of traditional crops often rely on a single application of pesticide to rid their crops of weeds and bugs. Organic crops require multiple applications. As a result, tractors on organic farms are used more than on traditional farms. Considering these economic factors, Pence asks how anyone can regard organic farming as a practical way to feed people with average incomes, much less the starving poor. In general, Pence views organic food as neither better nor worse than conventionally grown and genetically modified food, but simply impractical.

**Growing Organic Food**

The process of growing organic produce begins with farmers enriching their soil with natural fertilizers. Farmers control insects by encouraging or introducing creatures that prey on insects, by preventing destructive insects from mating, and by setting up various traps and barriers to keep pests away from crops. Farmers rotate their crops, plant overused fields with plants that enrich the soil, and weed their fields multiple times during a season. For stubborn pest infestations, farmers are permitted to use pesticides that occur naturally, such as rotenone and pyrethrins. Farmers feed their livestock organic food and send them out to pasture, where the animals' manure will fertilize the soil.

*Whole Foods, a leading retailer of organic and natural foods, has more than 250 locations in the United States and the United Kingdom.*

*Monsanto is a leading producer of genetically modified seeds. The company's headquarters are in St. Louis, Missouri.*

# POLITICS AND FOOD

The debate regarding genetically modified food extends beyond the United States and has a strong political aspect. Multinational corporations and other interest groups can exert a major influence on government food policy.

This can greatly affect the society being governed. Culture also factors into the political debate. Ethnic traditions that determine what and how people eat are powerful bonds.

Numerous people worry that large corporations have the ability to change a country's laws because they wield undue influence. Jennifer Kahn wrote in the April 1999 issue of *Harper's Magazine*:

> *Last year, Monsanto (whose board includes former U.S. Trade Representative Mickey Kantor) pressured the U.S. to threaten to cancel a trade agreement with New Zealand when the country said it would test and label transgenic food; direct pressure from Clinton, Gore, and four cabinet members also persuaded France to import Monsanto's corn.*[1]

Potentially, this gives corporations such as Monsanto the power to persuade governments to make laws that promote the interests of the corporations at home and abroad. Kahn explained such a situation regarding federal policy in the United States:

> *In 1992, when the FDA [Food and Drug Administration] wrote its policy on transgenic foods, it ruled that consumer labeling and safety testing were unneeded unless the genetic modification altered the*

**The Threat of Tariffs**

In 1999, U.S. Secretary of Agriculture Dan Glickman threatened to raise U.S. tariffs on European food if Europeans refused to import genetically modified soybeans and corn from the United States.

*nutritional content or posed a known health risk. The policy was written by an FDA deputy commissioner who had worked for Monsanto for seven years, and who does so again.* [2]

Many large corporations grow and process food. These businesses employ genetic engineers to experiment with ways to make seed better for farmers and food products more appealing to consumers. Major corporations that produce and sell genetically modified seeds and foods include Monsanto and DuPont in the United States, Syngenta in Switzerland, and AgrEvo in Germany.

INTRODUCTION TO EUROPE AND THE UNITED STATES

In 1996, Monsanto quietly introduced genetically modified soybeans to the United Kingdom. In August 1997, the lobbying activities of the U.S. government and U.S. corporations were instrumental in persuading the European Union to grant permission to import genetically modified soybeans throughout Europe. In addition, the ruling made labeling unnecessary for the genetically modified soybeans planted in 1996. Activists from European Green parties disagreed with the ruling and protested vigorously. Labeling is now required for genetically modified food in Europe.

Genetically modified organisms were introduced to the United States much the same way they were introduced to Europe. The companies creating them obtained permission from the appropriate government organizations to market genetically modified organisms. These included the U.S. Department of Agriculture, the Environmental Protection Agency, and the Food and Drug Administration. The large corporations did little to educate U.S. consumers about their activities, and U.S. reaction seemed indifferent compared to the European response.

## EUROPEAN OPPOSITION

Many Europeans fear that large U.S. corporations are forcing their products on other countries. Bioethics professor Gregory E. Pence attributes this negative response partly to the outbreak of bovine spongiform encephalopathy (BSE), or "mad cow disease," in England during the mid-1990s. Human consumption of meat infected with BSE can result in a fatal, incurable brain disorder known as vCJD. It is the human version of mad cow disease. By 1997, 23 people had died from vCJD. Europeans were shocked to learn that food they had always regarded as safe could kill them. There was no evidence that genetically modified crops were dangerous, but citizens' anxiety transferred to the genetically modified U.S. soybeans and corn being sent to Europe. Greenpeace International and other green groups advised the European public not to buy genetically modified food until its harmlessness was proven.

Pence notes that many European traditionalists have voiced strong objections to the creeping Americanization of their culture. They have watched as U.S.-based fast-food chains have moved into their countries. To many Europeans, genetically modified food seems to be the final decline of good taste. It represents an extreme end of the food spectrum, involving industrialized agriculture and processed food. Consequently, they supported their respective Green parties. The strong opposition led some European countries to temporarily ban the import of genetically modified food from the United States in 1998.

The front pages of newspapers in London, England, on March 21, 1996, focused on mad cow disease.

## U.S. Opposition

U.S. hostility toward genetically modified food was brought to the world's attention in 1999. The World Trade Organization (WTO) held a conference in Seattle, Washington, in November of that year. Thousands of demonstrators protested during the conference. Their aim was to shut it down.

The protestors claimed that the WTO represented the interests of powerful international corporations rather than those of poor, undeveloped nations. By furthering these interests, the WTO would keep the people of the third world dependent on industrialized nations and erode the democratic structures of developed nations. The protestors stated that unelected WTO officials secretly make important decisions that affect huge populations.

One of the Seattle demonstrators' key issues with the WTO was that member corporations developed and sold genetically modified food. The protestors noted that these corporations had put genetically modified food—which they refer to as "Frankenfoods"—on the market without proper labeling and without educating the public. They claimed that the corporations denied consumers the right to decide what kind of food they eat.

In response to such criticism, WTO members asserted that their aim was to help developing countries prosper. They claimed that all the advantages of genetically modified food can be enjoyed as much by poor countries as by prosperous ones. Despite the WTO's explanation, the demonstrators insisted that genetic engineers made modifications in plant genes to benefit farmers of industrialized nations rather than those of the third world. The opponents dismissed the famous golden rice developed to provide Asians with a source of much needed vitamin A. They contended that genetically modified organisms were an ineffective substitute for native plants that had once been more reliable sources of vitamin A and other nutrients.

## THE THIRD WORLD

Those who oppose the creation of genetically modified organisms worry that genetically modified plants and animals will destroy natural habitats that are important to the economies of developing countries. Organisms created to withstand weed

### Genetically Modified Organisms and Developing Countries

Edgar J. DaSilva is director of the Section of Life Sciences, Division of Basic and Engineering Sciences, United Nations Educational, Scientific and Cultural Organization. DaSilva said of genetically modified organisms (GMOs) in a report titled "GMOs and Development":

*Introduction of high yielding, drought tolerant, and early ripening varieties have led to impressive gains in maize production in Central and West Africa. . . . [T]here is development of supplementary and increased food markets. . . . The beneficial aspects of GMO crops and foods for developing countries are: improved nutritional quality and health benefits; an improvement in the quantity and quality of meat, milk, and livestock production; enhanced market possibilities and agronomic traits [characteristics of plants]; clean and safe methods for production of edible vaccines and drugs; wider environmental impact through development of clean technologies; reduction in dependence on costly fertilizers and herbicides . . . and no evidence that commercial transgenic crops contain new allergens other than those in normal foods.[3]*

killers, pests, and diseases could alter the balance of ecosystems. Opponents of genetically modified organisms highlight that it has been shown that genetically modified plants have cross-pollinated with closely related wild plants. This could cause foreign genes to spread in natural habitats with adverse ecological effects. Genetic engineers respond that they can prevent the spread of foreign genes by creating plants that do not develop viable seeds. Opponents counter that this practice forces poor farmers to buy new seeds every growing season from the companies that sell genetically modified plants. This adds costs to farmers' budgets that they cannot afford.

Genetic-engineering companies frequently point to the potential of plant engineering to enable farmers in poor countries to raise crops that can survive drought, resist pests and diseases, and thrive in challenging soils without expensive fertilizers and pesticides. Protestors reject these claims with the argument that these companies have thus far concentrated on improvements that help only wealthy farmers.

*A Missouri farmer plants Monsanto's Roundup Ready soybeans in July 2008.*

*Plant pathologist Norman Borlaug worked for many years to improve a range of plants with crossbreeding.*

# BENEFITS

The debate regarding genetically modified food goes beyond politics. Economics and quality are other parts of the argument. Proponents highlight the financial benefits of growing genetically modified crops. Some supporters point to the Green

Revolution of the 1960s as evidence that technology can solve economic problems.

## THE GREEN REVOLUTION

The Green Revolution was an agricultural movement that had its roots in the work of Norman Borlaug, a plant pathologist. He developed a variety of wheat resistant to wheat rust, a disease that was destroying wheat harvests in Mexico. Borlaug crossbred different strains of wheat until he bred one that could adapt to different growing conditions and withstand disease.

Borlaug worked for 16 years on developing new wheat varieties in Mexico. Later, he worked to improve other grains that serve as the staple crops of farmers in India, Africa, and Latin America. He and fellow scientists introduced herbicides and fertilizers never before used by the farmers in those areas. As a result, wheat and rice production in developing countries grew by approximately 75 percent between 1965 and 1980.

"With the technology that we now have available, and with the research information that's in the pipeline and in the process of being finalized to move into production, we have the know-how to produce the food that will be needed to feed the population of 8.3 billion people that will exist in the world in 2025."[1]

—Norman Borlaug, plant pathologist

ADVANCING BEYOND CROSSBREEDING

Many people argue that the agricultural achievements of genetic engineers will surpass those of the biologists who brought about the Green Revolution. Altering an organism's genetic makeup through genetic engineering is a faster and surer process than crossbreeding. Genetic engineering also can create traits that crossbreeding cannot. The genes available within a plant or animal species limit crossbreeding. Genetic engineering can use genes derived from other species. For example, genetic engineering can produce a modified plant using the genes of an animal that contains healing substances that no other plant of its species possesses.

In 1973, biochemists Stanley Cohen and Herb Boyer created the first genetically engineered organism. They took genes from *E. coli* bacteria, made them resistant to antibiotics, and then put them back into the bacteria. To prove that part of one organism's DNA could be joined to that of another organism, they added frog DNA to *E. coli* bacteria. These experiments did not result in helpful organisms, but they demonstrated that DNA could be successfully transferred between species.

*Monsanto soybeans grow in Argentina, the world's third-largest soybean producer and exporter, in 2003.*

Cohen and Boyer later created organisms that produced substances for the treatment and prevention of serious diseases. In 1980, the two men patented their methods for making human insulin and hepatitis B vaccine from genetically modified bacteria.

## Pest-resistant Plants

Many herbicides, or weed killers, damage the crops they are meant to protect. In the late 1980s, more than two dozen companies tried to

## Insecticidal Plants

Scientists are particularly optimistic about insecticidal plants, genetically engineered plants with built-in insecticides. They note that raising insect-resistant genetically engineered plants will save farmers money, work, and time. Unlike chemical insecticides that are sprayed on plants, genetically engineered protection is within the plant's tissues, not on its surface. Rain will not wash it away, and growth after spraying will not be vulnerable to pests.

In *Eat Your Genes*, Stephen Nottingham quoted figures showing the cost of producing and marketing a chemical insecticide as more than $25 million. In comparison, the development of an insect-resistant crop variety costs less than $1 million.

produce crop plants that would resist herbicides. Scientists believed crop yields would increase if genetic engineering was used to make crop plants resistant to weed killers. Monsanto found success with its genetically modified Roundup Ready soybeans. The soybeans resist large doses of a Roundup weed killer, a Monsanto product. When a crop is herbicide-resistant, the weeds that compete with the crop for resources can be sprayed even when the crop is at its most vulnerable. Weed control can be achieved more effectively and potentially with fewer herbicides.

Insecticides are designed to kill insect pests. To reduce the use of insecticides on crops, scientists have developed insect-resistant genetically modified plants. Belgium-based Plant Genetic Systems was one of the first companies to achieve this characteristic. Plant Genetic Systems introduced a toxin into a tobacco plant that killed tobacco hornworm. Cotton growers worldwide have reduced the amount of pesticide they spray by growing insect-resistant genetically modified varieties.

## EXTENDING FOOD'S SHELF LIFE

Scientists have also developed plants that produce food with a longer shelf life. This food remains tastier for longer periods, which reduces waste from spoilage. Experimenters at Calgene began by creating a special tomato. Many consumers prefer the flavor of tomatoes that are sun-ripened on the plant to that of tomatoes ripened off the plant. But sun-ripened tomatoes are expensive because they have a short shelf life. U.S. and British scientists developed a tomato that ripened more slowly on the vine. The tomato stayed at peak ripeness for a relatively long time after being picked.

In 1987, Calgene was granted the first U.S. patent for the genetically modified tomato. The Food and Drug Administration (FDA) allowed the marketing of this new tomato, the Flavr Savr, in the United States in May 1994. It was the first genetically modified food to receive FDA approval. However, the Flavr Savr tomato is no longer available to consumers because of several issues, including marketing and cultivation. In addition, the tomato

**Blue Genes for Blue Jeans**

Monsanto researchers are trying to produce cotton plants that yield blue fibers. Material made from these plants would not have to be dyed, and their color would not fade easily. Monsanto expects that jean manufacturers will be especially interested in denim made from the blue cotton.

was less flavorful than conventional tomatoes, and test rats who consumed the tomato developed unexplained lesions.

## PLANTS WITH HEALTH BENEFITS

Another goal of genetic engineers is to produce food plants with heightened health benefits. Protein is an important part of the human diet. Proteins are made up of chains of amino acids. Unfortunately, the protein in some food plants lacks certain essential amino acids. This can be a problem in vegetarian diets where only a restricted range of plants is available. Scientists can add genes for essential amino acids to food crops to make plant protein more nutritionally complete.

Also, scientists are developing vegetables and fruits that contain drugs and vaccines to cure or prevent illnesses. Bananas and potatoes are two examples. Researchers have genetically modified such fruits and vegetables to contain vaccines against illnesses such as Norwalk's disease and hepatitis B. This method for delivering vaccines is less expensive and more accessible than traditional methods, which makes them particularly beneficial to people in developing countries.

## SURVIVOR PLANTS

Plants can be designed to thrive in poor environmental conditions. Scientists have created plants that photosynthesize, or process sunlight into food, more efficiently than regular plants. Plants use nitrogen from the soil to aid photosynthesis. Scientists are trying to improve the ability of special bacteria to help plants obtain more nitrogen.

### The Globalist Belief System

Bioethics professor Gregory E. Pence calls people who consider free trade, capitalism, and technology the best means to equalize standards of living "globalists." Pence says of these capitalists:

*Globalists believe that better economics, not moral passion, raise standards of living, and in the long run, more people are helped by free world trade, specialization, investment of capital, and economies of scale than by international aid. . . . Globalists think that transfers of cash or food lack sustainability because altruism is a scarce resource. In contrast, human desire for profit is unlimited and more reliable [than altruism].*

Pence also points out that globalists believe that only specialized production can function effectively in today's world:

*For globalists, just as everyone shouldn't try to grow his own food, so each region shouldn't [grow its own food]. . . . The family farm . . . is an antique. Hunger will never be solved if every country tries to grow everything, especially on small, inefficient family plots.[2]*

A major focus is to create plants that can withstand environmental stresses, especially those associated with climate change. Plants are being produced with genes that help them withstand a variety of environments. These include drought, extremes of heat and cold—including frost—and flooding. Plants are also being produced to adapt to specific soil conditions, such as salt, pollution, or low quality, including contamination by harmful metals.

## Designer Animals

Companies worldwide are using gene transfer to give traits to animals that are helpful to human research. Research teams have created lab animals that are genetically prone to certain diseases. They can use these animals to help in the study of the effects of drugs and other chemicals on those diseases. Scientists also are producing cattle, sheep, chickens, and pigs that have faster growth rates, less body fat, and higher resistance to diseases. People in favor of genetically modified organisms find it difficult to understand why anyone would object to scientific advances with such benefits.

*A researcher examines genetically modified plants.*

*Protestors drew a question mark in a field in Oaxaca, Mexico, to object to transgenic contamination.*

# RISK AND EXPENSE

ritics of genetic engineering think its supporters are not properly examining its risks or the organizations that support its products. Many of these critics are not completely against genetic engineering. They feel the public should be cautious of genetically modified food that has not been adequately tested and regulated.

## MISTRUST OF POWERFUL CORPORATIONS

Challengers of genetic engineering do not trust the corporations that produce genetically modified crops. They believe these companies are more interested in making profits than in bettering the world. Critics point to the scandals involving Enron, a huge power company, and Halliburton, a corporation that deals in energy and military contracting. In order to protect their monetary interests, both companies have given false information to their investors and to the general public.

Critics claim that food corporations are reluctant to label the genetically modified food they market for the same reason. These opponents suspect the same motives might cause biotechnology companies to hide or misrepresent other kinds of information that consumers should have access to.

## NEGATIVE ASPECTS OF THE GREEN REVOLUTION

Few members of the general public know that the Green Revolution caused serious problems

**Agricultural Innovations in India**

M. S. Swaminathan is an agronomist and promoter of the Indian Green Revolution. In 1968, Swaminathan asked that agricultural innovations be introduced in India: "[T]he initiation of exploitative agriculture without a proper understanding of the various consequences of every one of the changes introduced into traditional agriculture, and without first building up a proper scientific and training base to sustain it, may only lead us, in the long run, into an era of agricultural disaster rather than one of agricultural prosperity."[1]

for farmers in developing nations. Although critics agree that the revolution helped developing countries initially, they stress that it ended by damaging these countries. By 1994, crop yields for poorer farmers had begun to level off or decline. The new strains of grain needed more chemical fertilizers and weed killers to continue to yield large harvests. As the levels of these chemicals accumulated over time, they polluted the soil and water sources. Insects and weeds became resistant to the pesticides. The new grains also needed more water than the original grains. Increased irrigation put a strain on water sources. Soon, the farmers could no longer afford to raise the new crops, and many had to sell their land.

## Risks of Plants with Built-in Pesticides

Prior to genetic engineering, there was a limit to the amount of weed killer that crop plants could absorb without being damaged. However, plants designed to resist herbicides do not die if sprayed heavily. Farmers may then overspray as an insurance strategy against weeds. According to Stephen Nottingham in *Eat Your Genes: How Genetically Modified Food Is Entering Our Diet*, agribusiness officials have requested government agencies to extend regulations regarding the limits of herbicide use. They also want regulations that will permit higher herbicidal residues in the plants. Nottingham points out that it is their business to sell weed killers, not to reduce the need to use them.

Overuse of herbicides can have several negative consequences. The ingredients of some weed killers are highly toxic to humans and could harm farm workers. For example, Monsanto's Roundup Ready is a glyphosate herbicide. This type of herbicide is the third most common cause of poisoning among farm workers. Herbicides also can kill desirable plants and make soil less suitable for growing crops.

## A Warning

In *Genetically Engineered Food: Changing the Nature of Nature*, Martin Teitel and Kimberly Wilson warn about a commonly used pesticide called *Bacillus thuringiensis* (Bt). Bt is extremely poisonous to caterpillars. It is used against several important agricultural pests. If sprayed on crops, it breaks down quickly and poses little danger to most nontarget insects. But if DNA from Bt is inserted into plants, the toxin is present continually in the leaves, and sometimes the pollen, of genetically modified crops. This constant presence increases the risk to nontarget insects, such as monarch butterflies.

*A sign in a cabbage field during pesticide spraying warns people not to enter.*

If genetically modified plants cross-pollinate with wild plants that are closely related to them, the weeds may also become resistant to herbicides. This means that more powerful weed killers must be used. Plants with genes programmed to kill pests can harm the environment. Because these genes change the chemistry of the plants, they can potentially harm nontarget organisms. For example, there has been concern that corn plants modified with a toxin lethal to caterpillar pests may inadvertently harm monarch butterflies. Harmful insects may become tolerant to the toxins manufactured by genetically modified plants quicker than spray insecticides because they are continuously present in the plant rather than intermittently applied.

## LIMITED NUTRITIONAL ENHANCEMENTS

Golden rice has not found complete acceptance. Critics claim that it was created to boost the genetically modified industry more than to nourish people. They contend there are better solutions to the problem of malnutrition. Green activists claim that many poor people starve in societies where food is plentiful. Instead of offering an expensive product such as designer rice, they believe it to be more practical to increase supplies of the available food and supplement citizens' diets with fortified food. Also, the best methods for cooking the rice are with steam or a microwave. Many poverty-stricken people do not have the equipment for proper preparation. Finally, a person may have to eat large quantities of modified plants to achieve recommended daily levels of nutrients.

**Golden Rice 2**

A second version of golden rice, Golden Rice 2, was launched in 2005. It has much higher levels of vitamin A than the original strain. It will probably complement, rather than replace, existing vitamin A supplementation programs.

Genetic engineers claim that food they have programmed to ripen slowly, such as the Flavr Savr tomato, can help the economies and diets of poor nations. With less spoilage, farmers and retailers can lower their prices. This will enable more people to buy fresh fruits and vegetables. Critics of genetically modified food are not convinced that such food is healthy. They stress that Flavr Savr tomatoes were approved for consumption and marketed despite the fact that they contained a gene resistant to antibiotics. These critics wonder what other hazards accompany the benefits of genetically modified food.

### Environmental Risks

Another argument against genetically modified organisms is that genetic engineering could harm the environment. Genes inserted into the DNA of plants can cause unpredictable changes within the plants. For example, genes meant to increase resistance to viruses have had the opposite effect. In 1996, farmers in Italy experienced a loss of tomato crops that had been programmed to resist viruses. This process resulted in a mutation that caused plants to develop lethal necrosis, the death of tissue cells in the plant.

Critics explain that even genetically modified organisms that develop as planned can cause unforeseen problems. Genetically modified plants that establish outside agricultural areas could outcompete other species if the foreign genes they contain give them a competitive advantage. This could adversely affect natural habitats.

Such plants could also damage the environment through the spread of their genes to closely related wild species. Insects can carry the foreign genes with pollen from one plant to

## The Threat of Monoculture

Martin Teitel and Kimberly Wilson, authors of *Genetically Engineered Food: Changing the Nature of Nature,* write that genetically modified farming will produce "monoculture" or "acres of genetically uniform crops."[2] Such crops are more vulnerable to insects and diseases than wild species. The 1845 potato famine in Ireland was due to the extensive growing of only one variety of potato that was not blight resistant. Teitel and Wilson warn that periodic genetically modified crop failures may occur due to pests and diseases. Scientists will need to create crops with greater pest resistance.

Teitel and Wilson also note that genetically modified crops give rise to less variety than do crops produced by traditional crossbreeding:

[G]enetic engineering allows for gene transfers between vastly unrelated species, such as fish and tomatoes. . . . In sexual reproduction, versions ("alleles") of the same genes are exchanged between plants. Because reproduction takes place via this exchange of differing versions of the same gene, . . . there is no risk, as there is in genetic engineering, of genes ending up in the wrong place, causing unexpected and potentially hazardous results.[3]

another. There have been incidents where herbicide resistance was transmitted to weeds that became immune to herbicides and developed more seeds than the original weeds could produce. This allowed them to spread quickly.

Most genetically modified animals can be kept in limited areas, but fish raised on fish farms can escape into open water. Fish genetically programmed to grow larger than conventional fish eat more and are better equipped to compete for food. These fish could outcompete and eventually replace native species.

Some opponents of genetically modified organisms believe their development must be stopped before they cause irreparable damage to the environment. Radical activists have destroyed labs where scientists conduct experiments and the fields where genetically modified crops are grown and tested. However, some critics can still see its benefits. But these skeptics want companies to have their new products properly tested by independent laboratories to ensure that they are indeed safe to introduce into the environment.

*A Greenpeace activist protests in Germany, where protestors are cutting off genetically modified plants.*

*Flasks of engineered seedlings grow in a laboratory.*

# TESTING

M ost people would welcome the benefits that proponents of genetic engineering claim. But they want assurance that these benefits actually exist without harmful side effects to consumers and the ecosystem. Many people are concerned about safety because the transferred foreign genes may not behave predictably. Experiments have demonstrated that this can occur.

In 1992, a German experimenter attempted to turn white petunias red by transferring a foreign gene into the petunias' genomes. The first generation of the modified petunia was red. Subsequent generations of the flower were white and a mixture of red and white. These variations in color were not consistent with the laws of crossbreeding. Scientists found that unusually hot weather had affected the gene that should have made the flowers red. This interaction between gene and environment meant that other more dangerous surprises might occur in the creation of genetically modified food.

However, genetic engineers claim that the results of genetically altering organisms are more predictable than the results of traditional crossbreeding. They stress that tens of thousands of genes determine a plant's characteristics. When botanists put the pollen from

"The only way to even begin to make a reliable safety assessment of a genetically engineered organism is to rigorously test for unintended and unexpected changes."[1]
—*John Fagan, professor of molecular biology and biochemistry, Maharishi University of Management*

**Lab Tests and Field Trials**

In *Genetically Engineered Food: Changing the Nature of Nature*, Martin Teitel and Kimberly Wilson note that lab tests and field trials have different purposes. Lab tests determine the safety of genetically modified organisms. Field trials determine whether they can thrive under natural conditions. There is no check to see if the traits of genetically modified organisms have changed as a result of interaction with the new environment. If they do not develop properly in the field, genetically modified organisms are not released commercially.

flowers of one plant strain onto the flowers of a plant strain from the same species, they cannot tell exactly what traits the offspring will have. But when genetic engineers insert foreign genes into organisms, they know that it will nearly always produce the trait they want. The environment or other factors may prevent the gene from functioning properly. But scientists insist that this can be corrected before the genetically modified organism leaves the laboratory—because testing is part of the experimental process.

The method genetic engineers use to test their results does not satisfy all critics. Some opponents say that scientists conducting the tests may not know all the factors involved in assessing new genetically modified organisms and food. Scientists counter that tests can give valuable information about the effectiveness and safety of genetically modified food when carried out thoroughly and with ingenuity, even if all the factors are not known.

## MONSANTO AND rBST

Monsanto's testing of bovine somatotropin (BST) reveals why it is important that new products should be tested by those who have no commercial interest in their success. Monsanto was one of the first of several companies to genetically modify BST. This hormone in dairy cattle controls growth, muscle development, and milk production.

The altered BSTs were called rBSTs. If a cow is injected with Monsanto's rBST every 14 or 28 days, the amount of milk produced will increase by 15 to 25 percent. Cows have been selectively bred to produce as much milk as is good for their health. Some researchers believe that pushing this limit by giving cows rBST may be harmful to both cows and humans. The overproduction of milk leads to mastitis—inflammation of the cow's udder—and the formation of large amounts of pus. A cow with mastitis will give discolored milk that contains unacceptable levels of pus.

After testing its version of rBST, Monsanto concluded that its product did not increase a cow's

*Wisconsin dairy farmer Jim Misna uses rBST to increase his herd's milk production.*

chances of developing mastitis. However, tests done by independent researchers Erik Millstone and Eric Brunner showed that cows treated with rBST were significantly more likely to develop mastitis than cows not treated with rBST. A review of Monsanto's tests revealed that the company's data was based on tests done for only a 28-week period, shorter than the 43-week period that the independent researchers used to show significant effects. Millstone and Brunner reasoned that the negative effects of rBST are most apparent toward the end of a cow's milk-production cycle. In 1994, Monsanto published data closer to that found by Millstone and Brunner.

## Arpad Pusztai and Rowett Research Institute

Opponents of genetically modified food suggest that the companies manufacturing these foods are highly selective with the test results they publish and try to prevent negative test results from being published. One often-quoted example concerns Arpad Pusztai, a noted expert on a group of chemicals called lectins. Rowett Research Institute had employed Pusztai for 36 years when he gave an interview on British television in August 1998. During the telecast, Pusztai mentioned that in one of his studies he had found a lectin gene in genetically modified potatoes that was toxic to lab rats. He expressed the opinion that the food testing done during one of his studies was inadequate. Soon after that interview, Rowett Research Institute dismissed Pusztai, seized his data, and distanced itself from his findings.

Some scientists believed that Rowett Research Institute's discrediting of Pusztai's work was warranted. They believed he had mistaken the cause of the rats' negative reaction to the genetically modified potatoes he was testing. Scientific consensus is that Pusztai could not produce substantial evidence for his conclusions, and these conclusions differed from those of other studies that were better documented. However, such studies are still infrequent. Food-research institutes rely on money from large corporations and do not want to be seen as going against the message the corporations are expressing.

## The FDA and Testing

The history of the Flavr Savr tomato developed

### A Call for More Careful Testing

During a televised interview in August 1998, research biologist Arpad Pusztai stated that genetically modified food was not as safe as it was advertised to be. He criticized testing procedures for genetically modified food. Pusztai had long been associated with Rowett Research Institute. Rowett immediately ended its relationship with Pusztai and forbade him from discussing the subject further. Pusztai gave an interview to *Frontline, India*, stating:

*They push something that is not properly tested and is potentially dangerous on to us and give us no choice. They have no right to do that. They have only the right to do scientific studies. When I started my experiments I was for GM [genetically modified] foods. But after what they did to me, my sympathies are with people campaigning against GM food. All I am saying is adequate studies have not been done. Because the companies when they released these things never tested them properly, it is our job to see what potential hazards we can have. It does not mean that, by definition, it must occur in nature, but it might occur. With irreversible GM technology this becomes even more important because you have no chance of having a remedy.[2]*

by Calgene illustrates how cautious the Food and Drug Administration (FDA) is in approving new genetically modified organisms in the United States. The FDA reviewed Calgene's test data on the tomato for nearly four years before pronouncing the tomato safe. Despite the lengthy review, some people suggest that the FDA never clearly established that the tomato was safe. For example, the federal agency did not eliminate the possibility that the Flavr Savr tomato might be a source of resistance to antibiotics.

Rebecca Goldburg is a senior scientist with Environmental Defense. She criticizes the FDA's reviewing procedure. According to Goldburg, the FDA left it up to Calgene to decide whether the tomato should be reviewed. Because there is no mandatory approval process for genetically engineered foods, Goldburg fears that not all companies

"The FDA had never been asked to declare a tomato safe, and it wasn't sure it wanted to start. . . . Simply put, no one could prove that a genetically engineered tomato was safe, because there existed no way to prove that any traditional food was safe. Tomatoes, potatoes, coffee, and all other traditional foods were simply assumed to be safe or at least safe enough, because humans had eaten them for a long time and survived."[3]
—*Daniel Charles, author*
Lords of the Harvest: Biotech, Big Money, and the Future of Food

**Radical Greenpeace Activists**

When Ingo Potrykus developed golden rice, it was rumored that Greenpeace activists might disrupt test plantings of the rice. Potrykus warned Greenpeace, "If you plan to destroy test fields to prevent responsible testing and development of Golden Rice for the humanitarian purpose, you will be accused of contributing to a crime against humanity."[4]

will offer their products for FDA inspection.

By 2008, many scientists claimed that fears of disastrous effects from genetically modified organisms were without grounds. They stressed that no health problems have been traced to genetically modified food in the 12 years it has been on the market and consumed by millions of people. ⌐

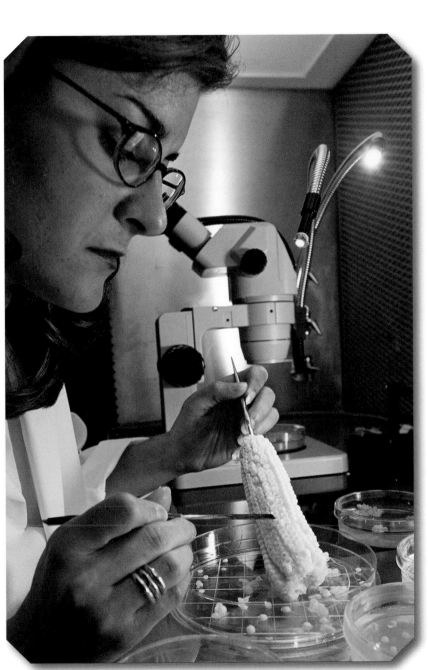

A Monsanto worker extracts corn embryos to develop
a genetically modified crop.

U.S. biotechnology company Biogen Idec had an 84 percent increase in its 2007 fourth-quarter profits.

# BUSINESS PRACTICES

Leaders of biotechnology and food corporations readily admit that their companies—like most businesses—strive for profits. These leaders reason that this want spurs innovation. When biotechnology corporations bring their

goods and services to developing countries, they
believe they are introducing technological skills
and the entrepreneurial spirit to these third-world
populations.

Some critics believe corporations manipulate and
deceive the general public, especially considering
the pressure these businesses exert on governments.
Through this influence, biotechnology corporations
can make independent farmers in developing
countries dependent on multinational corporations
for patented seed that needs to be sprayed with
branded pesticides.

## Progress versus Nostalgia

Supporters of genetic engineering consider such
criticism prejudiced against progress and practicality.
They see anticorporate people as nostalgic for the
days when families raised organic crops for local
markets and their own use.

Those who favor biotechnology believe farmers
in third-world countries should raise genetically
engineered crops instead of traditional varieties.
Growing genetically modified plants could result
in increased harvest yields, less pesticide use, and
enhanced nutritional products. Teaching farmers

in developing countries about progressive farming techniques can help them make their farms less labor intensive and more profitable. The farmers can then send their children to school instead of keeping them home to help work the farm. This will help them lead healthier, more fulfilling lives.

Opponents believe genetic engineering riskier and more wasteful than conventional breeding. Supporters counter that new organisms made by gene insertion are safer for consumers and the environment since scientists have more control over the genes involved in the process. Moreover, these organisms are rigorously tested before being released into nature.

## Terminator Genes

Critics of biotechnology businesses are concerned that company leaders take advantage of their clients. One business practice in dispute is Monsanto's requirement that its customers buy new seeds from the company every year. Opponents think farmers have always had the right to save the seeds from their harvested plants. Biotechnology supporters respond that Monsanto and similar companies must ensure that their intellectual property is not stolen. To do this, companies require farmers who buy their seeds to sign a contract stating they will not use the seeds from harvested crops.

Monsanto has acquired the genetic engineering technology to make plants that produce sterile seeds using terminator genes. Monsanto leaders stress that lower production costs, less damage to the ecology, and increased crop yields make it worthwhile to farmers to buy the sterile seeds. Opposition to seeds that produce sterile plants continues. Monsanto announced that it would not market seeds that produce sterile plants until it had better public approval. As of 2008, Monsanto had not commercialized its terminator genes.

"For such globalist thinkers, rising wealth broadly distributed in undeveloped countries would mean better medical care, cleaner air, healthier water, and better all-around living standards. Indeed, some delegates from poor countries claimed WTO [World Trade Organization] protestors 'cared more about turtles than the people of poor countries.'"[1]

—*Gregory E. Pence,*
*author,*
Designer Food: Mutant Harvest or Breadbasket of the World?

## PATENTS

Corporations obtain patents for their work. A patent is an official approval that gives inventors an exclusive right to make, use, or sell their inventions. This right is granted for a fixed period of time. When that time has elapsed, information about how

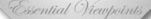

*A farmer holds Monsanto's Roundup Ready soybean seeds.*

an invention is made becomes available for general use. Biotechnology businesses invest a great deal of money in the development of genetically modified plants and animals. Getting full patent protection to cover the genetic engineering techniques used and the seed sold has been vital for the financial viability of genetically modified crops.

Until the mid-1900s, obtaining a patent for plants and seeds was difficult. Traditional patent law makes a distinction between inventions that spring from a person's intellect or imagination and those that come from natural life forms, such as plants and seeds. Plants bred through traditional methods have been covered by Plant Breeder's Rights since the 1930s. Initially, only new varieties of crops that were produced by manipulating mutations and are propagated asexually could be patented.

In 1970, the United States Plant Variety Protection Act gave U.S. breeders limited rights over the seeds of new varieties they had developed from sexually reproducing plants. Farmers could not sell seeds produced by the new hybrids, but they could store the new seeds and use them to raise crops. Because specially developed hybrids were considered products of nature, their breeders still could not claim rights over their creations.

At first, similar restrictions held for patenting genetically engineered organisms. But this changed toward the end of the twentieth century. In the late 1970s, General Electric Company designed a new strain of the bacterium *Pseudomonas* to clean up oil slicks by digesting the oil. In 1980, the U.S. Supreme Court declared the organism to be a unique human invention—not a product of nature—and ordered the U.S. Patent and Trademark

Office to grant General Electric a patent for the
new strain of bacterium. Between 1980 and 1984,
Stanford University and the University of California
received patents for Boyer and Cohen's development
of insulin and vaccine-producing bacteria. The
patents applied to most of the genetic engineering
techniques being used at that time.

## Do Patents Legalize Monopolies?

These breakthroughs in patent law set the stage
for greater changes. They encouraged corporations
that developed and sold genetically modified
organisms to apply for patents and to challenge the
government's refusal to grant them. Within a few
years, multinational companies had little trouble
obtaining patents for genetically modified organisms
worldwide. Opponents of genetically modified
organisms are concerned about what this might mean
for the future of agriculture and consumers.

On March 2, 1994, the European company
Agracetus gained a 17-year patent over all the
genetically modified soybeans in Europe, regardless
of the methods used to develop them. Monsanto
and an international coalition of public interest
groups brought suit against the European Patent

Office. The two groups were on the same side of the issue—the patent was too broad—but for different reasons. Monsanto believed the patent would "have a chilling effect on research" and the coalition argued that the patent could "threaten future world food supplies."[2] Agracetus went on to acquire patents for genetically modified cotton. It also applied for patents for genetically modified rice, groundnuts, and corn. When Monsanto bought Agracetus in 1996, it gained that company's rights over these genetically modified crops.

### Patent Laws Favor Huge Biotech Companies

In *Safe Food: Bacteria, Biotechnology, and Bioterrorism*, Marion Nestle expresses concern about the scope of ownership that patents have granted to biotech companies:

*Control of the "discoveries" of genetic engineering creates distrust because of the extraordinary breadths of some of the patents. One . . . grants exclusive rights to all forms of bioengineered cotton; another covers all uses of reverse genes such as those used to create the Calgene tomato; . . . Competitors of the companies holding such patents find their scope stunning. . . . Such concerns are quite justifiable. For example, just four companies control 65 percent of the patents owned by the top 30 companies working on transgenic seeds: Pharmacia (which in 2002 owned Monsanto, Calgene, and other agricultural biotechnology companies), DuPont (Pioneer Hi-Bred), Syngenta (Zenica, Novartis, and others), and Dow Chemical (Mycogen). Monsanto . . . alone owns more than 100 patents for the processes used to construct transgenic corn and soybeans.[3]*

"The term monopoly takes on new power when one imagines a company owning major portions of our food supply—the one thing that every single person now and into the future will always need to buy."[4]

—*Martin Teitel and Kimberly A. Wilson, authors,* Genetically Engineered Food: Changing the Nature of Nature

Large multinational corporations claim that the general population benefits from genetically modified organisms. Opponents state that trade organizations make rules that favor the corporations rather than the people. For example, in 1997, the World Trade Organization (WTO) backed U.S. efforts to make India change its patent laws to conform to those of multinational corporations. That same year, the European Parliament approved a draft proposal granting patents to genetically modified organisms.

Granting patents for life forms can give a corporation exclusive control over all genetically modified varieties of an entire crop species. This might lead to that group taking complete control over most research involving an essential food plant. Critics of multinational corporations believe trade and patent laws would result in food monopolies. This would destroy healthy competition and disrupt the balance of power among the nations of the world and the ecosystem.

*Canadian farmer Percy Schmeiser went to court in January 2004
for infringing Monsanto's patent on a plant.*

*In India, neem and turmeric are ground for a traditional treatment paste.*

# CULTURE, RELIGION, AND HUMANITY

*S*ome opponents of genetic engineering express cultural, religious, and humanitarian concerns. These critics believe multinational agribusinesses have occasionally plundered vulnerable cultures, showed disrespect for religious values, and caused animal suffering. Some of these concerns stem as much from unfair business practices as from the type of products being made and sold.

## BIOPIRACY

Biopiracy occurs when prospectors from companies go to developing countries to find plants used by the native people as food, pesticide, or medication, and then exploit their findings without the consent of that country. After learning how native farmers process a plant to make it useful, prospectors may vary the process enough to be able to claim the process as their own invention. Or they may isolate the genes that give a plant its value for use in genetic engineering. The agribusinesses then claim that patent laws give them the right to own the plant's genes or the process that makes the plant's qualities valuable.

**Turmeric**

Turmeric is a powder made from the roots of *Curcuma longa*, a plant native to India and Southeast Asia. U.S. researchers obtained a patent for a method of using turmeric to heal wounds. Indians challenged this patent on the grounds that the plant's healing power had been known for centuries. They proved this claim by producing an ancient text that discusses this use of turmeric. The U.S. Patent and Trademark Office revoked the patent.

If these companies acquire ownership of the genes or the technology, they potentially have the power to prevent native people from freely using one of their traditional resources.

One case of biopiracy involved the neem tree. The tree grows throughout India and provides Indians with a variety of benefits. They eat its leaves to strengthen their immune systems, massage their gums with its twigs, and use its bark and seeds to kill insects and fungi. Teams of corporate scientists worked out formulas for making disinfectants and pesticides from the neem tree. The corporations then applied for patents for these formulas.

W. R. Grace is a multinational company based in the United States. In 1995, the company obtained a patent for the antifungal agents in the neem's seeds and bark. This meant that Indians, the people who first discovered and developed this property, now had to pay W. R. Grace to use the neem as a means of killing fungi.

The Indians were outraged. Not only did they have to pay another country to use one of their own resources, they also lost a part of their cultural heritage. Under the combined leadership of Indian environmentalist Vandana Shiva and Belgian

Minister of State Magda Aelvoet, Indians fought W. R. Grace's patent. Ten years later, on March 8, 2005, the European Patent Office revoked W. R. Grace's patent. The decision was based on the argument that W. R. Grace had not discovered the fungicidal property of the neem tree and the manufacture of the fungicide was a "prior art" practiced by Indians for centuries. It was the first time a patent had been denied for this reason.

### Stealing Cultural Heritages

In *Genetically Engineered Food: Changing the Nature of Nature*, authors Martin Teitel and Kimberly A. Wilson describe biopiracy:

*In more recent times, plant breeding has been taken on by big universities and corporations. These production-oriented entities have searched the globe for the raw materials of their plant-breeding experiments. . . . [They] travel to distant countries, usually the nonindustrialized lands where the food plants originated. The collectors bring back samples on which to base their new varieties. Although the plants that are "discovered" on these ex-peditions might be the result of thousands of years of patient community effort, the collectors just take and use [them].*

*The problem arises when the universities, governments, or corporations that get the plants from other nations place strains of those plants, or processes us-ing those plants, under patent. With the stroke of a pen, . . . the common heritage of some distant people or tribe becomes the exclusive property of those who took it. Even the originators of the plant could risk infringement if they clashed with the patent holders in how they used their own foodstuffs.[1]*

*Dr. Vandana Shiva has campaigned to keep Monsanto from what she sees as an overtaking of India's centuries-old agricultural practices.*

## Gene Theft

Corporate prospectors also collect the seeds of valuable plant strains. One British company has obtained patents for the flavor gene of a West African cacao tree. If the company uses the gene to make artificial chocolate, it might no longer be necessary for the manufacturers of chocolate to import cocoa beans from Africa. Likewise, other multinational companies might use caffeine genes from coffee beans to make artificial coffee. This could put African or Latin American growers out of work.

Developing artificial chocolate and coffee in this way could result in a drastic reduction of income developing countries earn from the sales of cocoa beans and coffee.

Perhaps financial loss suffered by poor countries is the most urgent problem caused by biopiracy. In *Food, Inc.: Mendel to Monsanto—The Promise and Perils of the Biotech Harvest*, Peter Pringle writes, "A report commissioned by Christian Aid estimated that biopiracy was costing third-world countries 4.5 billion [dollars] a year."[2] Even multinational corporations admit that bioprospecting damages developing nations. These companies agree that patent laws should be better defined to prevent them from being applied too broadly. Financial arrangements that give developing countries a share of the profits derived from the use of genetic material are becoming more common.

## Religious Issues

Genetically modified organisms also raise issues regarding religion.

**Nature Will Revenge Itself**

Some people have a reverence for nature that borders on a religious feeling. Some nature lovers believe that nature keeps itself in balance best when humans do not interfere with its processes. These people are appalled by genetic engineers who try to force on plants and animals qualities they could not develop naturally. They feel that nature will avenge itself on humans by making Earth uninhabitable.

The transference of genes from animals to plants can raise problems for people who want to follow the dietary laws of their faith. For example, Jewish and Islamic dietary laws prohibit eating pork.

Some Christian fundamentalists believe that genetic engineers are defying God. They stress that God set clear rules for farmers that are in the Bible. These rules forbid sowing different seeds in one field, breeding one animal with a different kind, or wearing a garment made of both linen and wool. Strict religious objectors to genetic engineering argue that these biblical restrictions apply to mixing the genes from different organisms. In addition, many religious objectors feel that genetic engineers are committing a sin worse than defiance of agricultural rules. By manipulating DNA, these scientists are trying to take God's role of creating life.

"Thus, there is no room in God's creation for man to step in and start modifying DNA by cross transplanting the genes from one organism or species into the DNA of another. . . . Such alteration of species specificity is a serious violation of God's natural order, and I believe it to be a corruption of life and an abomination unto the LORD."[3]
—*Greg Ciola, editor and publisher of* Crusador, *a health newsletter rooted in the Bible*

## Humanitarian Concerns

Other critics of genetic engineering feel that scientists have not given enough thought to the suffering of genetically modified animals. Genetic engineering has brought about new risks to livestock and other domestic animals. Some genetic programming intended to make animals more profitable to farmers can also bring about serious health problems for the animals. Many animal activists have cited the Beltsville pigs as evidence that genetic modification can cause extreme suffering. In the mid-1980s, researchers at the U.S. Department of Agriculture in Beltsville, Maryland, inserted a gene for human growth hormone into embryo pigs. The scientists had hoped to increase the growth rate of the pigs and enhance their value as food animals. The pigs were born with a number of defects, including severe arthritis, blindness, and spinal deformities. Some humane groups oppose all genetic-modification experiments on food animals. They argue that food production in developed countries is more than sufficient and hurting animals in hopes of getting even more food from them is unnecessary.

Animals are designed for more than food uses. They are also designed for medical uses. Harvard University received a patent for developing a type of experimental mouse, OncoMouse, in 1988. The mice in this group were genetically designed

"While genetically engineering farm animals to increase bone strength or reduce reception to pain, for example, may improve animal well-being, the broad use of such technology would be unlikely to result in a reduction of suffering."[4]

—*United States Humane Society*

to be unusually susceptible to cancer. The scientists use the mice to test chemicals suspected of being carcinogenic, which can cause cancer. At the time, the U.S. Patent and Trademark Office did not easily grant patents for genetically modified animals. Initially, it refused to do so for OncoMouse because the benefits of the experiment did not outweigh the suffering of the animals involved. But Harvard appealed, and a patent was granted. This decision paved the way for other genetically modified animals.

U.S. laws for the treatment of experimental animals are not clear-cut. This is primarily because two systems with different rules are involved in regulation. The U.S. Animal Welfare Act monitors the treatment of all farm animals used as experiment subjects. The U.S. Food and Drug Administration (FDA) regulates the treatment of animals that have already been modified for medical use. The FDA uses the same criteria for the care of animals and bacteria. U.S. regulations have allowed the creation of large numbers of genetically modified animals.

*Quechua Indians in Peru have grown the maca plant for centuries. Peru created its National Anti-Biopiracy Commission to prevent biopiracy.*

*Students and activists gather outside the Thai Ministry of Agriculture in July 2006 to demonstrate against genetically modified papaya.*

# THE FUTURE OF GENETIC ENGINEERING

ommercial genetically modified crops have been grown worldwide since approximately 1996. According to a 2008 report by the International Service for the Acquisition of Agri-Biotech Applications (ISAAA), the global area on which these crops were raised exceeded 1.7 billion acres (688 million ha) in 2007. This was a 12 percent increase from 1996. The ISAAA report noted that many of the world's farmers have planted genetically modified crops with two or more beneficial traits, which is referred to as stacked traits. The report claimed that the factor of stacked traits increases the virtual increase in global land area planted with genetically modified crops from 12 percent to 22 percent from 1996 to 2007.

The ISAAA report also stated that a recent survey estimates that the accumulative global economic benefit of these crops during the years from 1996 to 2006 was $16.5 billion for developing countries and $17.5 billion for industrial countries. The estimated reduction in pesticides for that same period is 318,565 tons (289,000 tonnes) of active ingredients. This totals a 15.5 percent reduction in the environmental impact of pesticide use on the genetically modified crops.

### GRAIN on the ISAA

GRAIN is an international organization based in Barcelona, Spain, that "promotes the sustainable management and use of agricultural biodiversity based on people's control over genetic resources and local knowledge."[1] According to GRAIN, "ISAAA receives support from a number of institutions and biotech companies, including the Rockefeller Foundation, USAID, Novartis, Monsanto and AgrEvo."[2] GRAIN wrote of the ISAAA, "[It] is constrained from the start by a very narrow framework: all of ISAAA's activities must encourage and deploy biotechnology in the target country."[3]

According to the ISAAA report, more than 90 percent of the global total of 12 million biotechnology farmers in 2007 consisted of small farmers in developing countries. This was a sharp increase from the number of poor farmers in developing countries in 2006. The ISAAA report cites this increase as evidence that genetic engineering has substantial social benefits.

## TESTING IN THE UNITED STATES

In the United States, the Food and Drug Administration (FDA) determines whether food is safe for humans and animals to eat. In 1992, the FDA ruled that genes used to modify food plants are not food additives. Therefore, the FDA does not have to review genetically modified food before it is marketed. For the most part, however, manufacturers have reviewed their test data on genetically modified products with the FDA before putting them on the market.

Manufacturers and the FDA check genetically modified food to verify

> "I challenge those who oppose GM [genetically modified] crops for emergent farmers to stand up and deny my fellow farmers and me the benefit of earning this extra income and more than sufficient food for our families."[4]
> —*Richard Sitole, chairperson, Hlabisa District Farmers' Union in South Africa*

*A label from a box of Erewhon Crispy Brown Rice Cereal advertises that the product contains no genetically modified ingredients.*

that the foreign genes do not cause allergies or harm consumers. Their evaluations cannot ensure that the new food is perfectly safe, but the evaluations determine whether or not the beneficial or harmful effects are equivalent to those of unmodified food on the market.

## Labeling

Critics feel U.S. regulations on genetically modified foods do not effectively safeguard consumers. They have requested that companies be required to label these products. The companies and regulatory authorities argue that genetically modified food is "substantially equivalent" to comparable food produced without genetic engineering and should be labeled no differently. However, critics argue that mandatory labeling would at least allow consumers to make more informed choices about what they eat and how it is produced, as is the case with organic food.

During the 2000 World Trade Organization talks in Montreal, Canada, U.S. food corporations compromised on the policy of labeling goods sold abroad. They did not agree to separate genetically modified food from conventional food as the Europeans had asked. However, they did consent to label shipments of mixed genetically modified food and conventional food as containing genetically modified organisms. As of summer 2008, the U.S. government had not yet required food companies to label products sold in the United States.

## Effects of Genetic Engineering

Some people feel that the debate over labeling has become irrelevant. They stress that considerable processed food contains genetically modified ingredients not identified on the package. They further note that such products have been marketed unlabeled for more than a decade. Proponents of marketing unlabeled genetically modified food claim that these products have done no significant harm.

Environmental issues are still being debated. Critics of genetic engineering stress that genes from genetically modified organisms have already spread throughout the world and entered the genomes of native plants. For example, in 2002, it was found that ancient strains of corn in Oaxaco, Mexico, now contain genes from genetically modified U.S. corn that was being grown in fields near the traditional strains of corn.

### Basic Questions

In *Safe Food: Bacteria, Biotechnology, and Bioterrorism*, Marion Nestle summarizes some of the major viewpoints on the genetic engineering issue:

*Food technology is a huge business, and huge profits are at stake. To survive, the industry must make products that farmers or the public will buy. Politics enters the picture because other stakeholders in the food system have different agendas and hold different values. Scientists want to work on challenging problems that might produce health or economic gains, and, as a necessary benefit, research funding. Government regulators want to ensure that foods are safe, but they also want to avoid congressional intervention and industry lawsuits. As consumers, we all want food that is safe (or safe enough), but many of us are concerned with social issues. Food biotechnology is political because basic questions—Who benefits? Who decides? Who controls?—require societal resolution and cannot be decided solely by the methods of science.[5]*

## Artificial Life?

The development of genetically modified plants was once seen as the cutting edge of genetic engineering. However, the procedures involved are now conducted routinely in laboratories around the world. Genetics research continues to advance and raises new issues concerning environmental and human safety as well as new ethical and moral questions.

**Corn in Oaxaca, Mexico**

In November 2001, Ignacio Chapela and David Quist published an article in the scientific journal *Nature* revealing that indigenous corn in Oaxaca, Mexico, was contaminated with DNA from genetically modified corn in the United States. The biotechnology industry has been working to discredit the research by the two scientists from the University of California at Berkeley. Many editorials and articles against the research have been traced to Monsanto's public relations firm. Pressure and criticism from a small group of influential biotechnology supporters caused *Nature* to withdraw the article in April 2002.

J. Craig Venter is a leading contributor to the mapping of the human genome. In 2007, Venter and his team of researchers created a DNA molecule that represents the complete genome of a parasitic microbe called *Mycoplasma genitalium*. This achievement is the closest scientists have come to creating artificial life. The next step to reaching this goal is inserting the genetic material into the empty shell of a nonliving cell. Venter and his colleagues hope that doing this will result in a new organism that can replicate itself.

The possibility of a human-made life-form horrifies some people. They fear that scientists might lose control of the artificial microbes that might take on dangerous characteristics. Critics also point out that a scientist might create organisms that could be used as deadly weapons. Some worry that a single biotechnology company might dominate the world by patenting the building blocks of life.

Venter and his colleagues argue that the world cannot afford to dismiss such important new breakthroughs. They may pave the way to the production of nonpolluting fuels, the breakdown of toxic wastes, and the absorption of carbon dioxide from the atmosphere to help counter the effects of climate change.

## THE DEBATE CONTINUES

The debate over genetically modified organisms has raised a number of questions that have not yet been answered to the satisfaction of either side. There are many issues regarding the benefits of genetic engineering and how much it can positively affect the world and its people. It is not yet known if genetic engineering can help reduce such global problems as poverty, the energy crisis, and climate change. And there are concerns about regulation and labeling. Consumers want to feel confident in the safety of the food they buy and eat, while producers want to market their genetically modified food products freely and easily.

The issue of ethics arises when debating genetically modified organisms, and it must be negotiated with sensitivity. Companies want to protect their intellectual property, but doing so presents the potential of creating monopolies of necessary goods or pirating the cultural heritages of other nations. There are also religious concerns, including the belief that genetic scientists are playing God.

Genetic engineering offers solutions to many world problems and opens opportunities for individuals to improve their lives. It is uncertain to many, however, whether these advantages can be realized without causing more serious problems. The value of debating this question is that the two sides might reach compromises that fulfill the technology's promises and avoid its pitfalls.

*Growing genetically modified organisms, such as fruits and vegetables, is an ongoing debate.*

# TIMELINE

## 1953

On April 25, James Watson and Francis Crick publish their paper on the double-helix structure of DNA in *Nature*.

## 1962

The Green Revolution begins with the planting of high-yielding wheat varieties in Mexico.

## 1962

Rachel Carson publishes *Silent Spring*.

## 1980

The U.S. Supreme Court orders a U.S. patent granted to General Electric for its organism that cleans up oil slicks.

## 1986

The U.S. Environment Protection Agency approves the release of the first genetically engineered crop—a virus-resistant tobacco plant.

## 1987

Calgene receives the first U.S. patent for a genetically modified tomato, the Flavr Savr.

| 1970 | 1973 | 1980 |
|------|------|------|
| The U.S. Plant Variety Protection Act gives U.S. breeders limited rights to seeds of new varieties they created from sexually reproducing plants. | Stanley Cohen and Herb Boyer create the first genetically modified organism. | Cohen and Boyer are granted a U.S. patent for creating a genetically modified organism that makes insulin. |

| 1990 | 1992 | 1994 |
|------|------|------|
| Congress passes the Organic Foods Production Act. | The FDA rules that genes used to modify food plants are not food additives, so labeling is not always needed. | Agracetus gains a 17-year patent over all the genetically modified soybeans in Europe, regardless of the methods used to develop them. |

# TIMELINE

| 1994 | 1995 | 1996 |
|------|------|------|
| Calgene's Flavr Savr tomato becomes the first genetically modified food to receive FDA approval. | U.S.-based W. R. Grace obtains a patent for the antifungal agents in the seeds and bark of the neem tree. | U.S. seed company Monsanto introduces genetically modified soybeans into the United Kingdom in April. |

| 1999 | 1999 | 2003 |
|------|------|------|
| Peter Beyer and Ingo Potrykus develop golden rice. | Demonstrations take place against the World Trade Organization during a November conference in Seattle. | Researchers find that ancient strains of corn in Oaxaca, Mexico, contain genes from genetically modified U.S. corn growing nearby. |

## 1997

European Union accepts a recommendation that patents be granted to genetically modified organisms.

## 1998

Some European countries impose bans on the import of genetically modified food.

## 1998

Monsanto discovers that it is possible to produce sterile seeds for their genetically modified crops.

## 2005

On March 8, the European Patent Office revokes W. R. Grace's patent on the fungicidal property of the neem tree.

## 2007

J. Craig Venter and his research team create a DNA molecule that represents the complete genome of a parasitic microbe.

## 2007

The global area on which genetically modified crops were raised exceeds 1.7 billion acres (688 million ha).

# ESSENTIAL FACTS

## AT ISSUE

### Opposed

❖ Genetically engineering organisms for food and medicine is an expensive and impractical way to help the poor.

❖ Genetically modified food may harm animals and humans.

❖ Genetically modified crops may harm the environment.

❖ Genetic engineering is offensive to various religious groups.

❖ By acquiring patents for genetically modified products, businesses might obtain monopolies over goods necessary to live.

### In Favor

❖ Genetic engineering can produce more nutritious food and inexpensive medicines, which will be helpful to the poor.

❖ Creating plants and animals that can withstand environmental stresses and resource shortages can reduce pollution and make them more adaptable to climate change.

❖ Producing pest-resistant plants can lessen the need for pesticides and reduce environmental damage.

❖ Genetically modified plants can help farmers with less acreage yield more and better crops.

❖ Genetically modified food can have a longer shelf life to enhance taste and reduce waste.

## CRITICAL DATES

### 1970

The U.S. Plant Variety Protection Act gave U.S. breeders limited rights over the seeds of new varieties they had developed from sexually reproducing plants.

### 1980

Stanley Cohen and Herb Boyer were granted a U.S. patent for a genetically modified organism that makes insulin. Also, the U.S.

Supreme Court declared General Electric's organism that cleaned oil slicks to be a unique human invention and ordered the U.S. Patent and Trademark Office to grant General Electric a patent.

### 1992

The U.S. Food and Drug Administration ruled that genes used to modify food plants are not food additives. The manufacturer of a genetically modified product does not need approval for marketing it. Also, a genetically modified product does not need to be labeled as genetically modified unless its safety and nutrition are well below those of conventional food.

### 1994

On March 2, Agracetus gained a 17-year patent over all the genetically modified soybeans in Europe, regardless of the methods used to develop them.

### 1997

European Union accepted the European Commission's recommendation that patents be granted to genetically modified organisms on the grounds that they were human inventions.

## Quotes

"[T]he initiation of exploitative agriculture without a proper understanding of the various consequences of every one of the changes introduced into traditional agriculture, and without first building up a proper scientific and training base to sustain it, may only lead us, in the long run, into an era of agricultural disaster rather than one of agricultural prosperity."—*M. S. Swaminathan, agronomist and promoter of the Indian Green Revolution*

"I challenge those who oppose GM [genetically modified] crops for emergent farmers to stand up and deny my fellow farmers and me the benefit of earning this extra income and more than sufficient food for our families."—*Richard Sitole, chairperson, Hlabisa District Farmers' Union in South Africa*

# ADDITIONAL RESOURCES

## SELECT BIBLIOGRAPHY

Nestle, Marion. *Safe Food: Bacteria, Biotechnology, and Bioterrorism*. Berkeley, CA: University of California Press, 2003.

Nottingham, Stephen. *Eat Your Genes: How Genetically Modified Food Is Entering Our Diet*. New York: Zed Books Ltd., 2003.

Pence, Gregory E. *Designer Food: Mutant Harvest or Breadbasket of the World?* New York: Rowman & Littlefield Publishers, Inc., 2002.

Pringle, Peter. *Food, Inc.: Mendel to Monsanto—the Promises and Perils of the Biotech Harvest*. New York: Simon & Schuster, 2003.

Teitel, Martin, and Kimberley A. Wilson. *Changing the Nature of Nature: What You Need to Know to Protect Yourself, Your Family, and Our Planet*. Rochester, VT: Park Street Press, 2001.

## FURTHER READING

Altieri, Miguel. *Genetic Engineering in Agriculture: The Myths, Environmental Risks, and Alternatives*. Oakland, CA: FoodFirst, 2001.

McCuen, Marnie J., ed. *Redesigning Creation: Debating the Biotech Revolution*. Hudson, WI: GE McCuen Publications, 2000.

Walker, Mark, and David McKay. *Unravelling Genes: A Layperson's Guide to Genetic Engineering*. St. Leonards, N.S.W., Australia: Allen and Unwin, 2000.

## WEB LINKS

To learn more about genetically modified foods, visit ABDO Publishing Company online at **www.abdopublishing.com**. Web sites about the genetically modified food debate are featured on our Book Links page. These links are routinely monitored and updated to provide the most current information available.

## For More Information

For more information on this subject, contact or visit the following organizations.

**The Children's Museum of Indianapolis**
3000 North Meridian Street, Indianapolis, IN 46208-4716
317-334-3322
www.childrensmuseum.org/themuseum/biotech/index.htm
The museum's Biotechnology Learning Center educates
elementary and middle school students and their families about
biotechnology, its history, and its effect on food and plants.

**Massachusetts Institute of Technology**
MIT Museum, Building N51, 265 Massachusetts Avenue,
Cambridge, MA 02139
617-253-5927
web.mit.edu/museum/exhibitions/learninglab.html
The museum's Learning Lab: The Cell exhibit is designed for
middle school and high school students. It provides information
about DNA and protein synthesis.

**Museum of Science and Industry**
57th Street and Lake Shore Drive, Chicago, IL 60637
773-684-1414
www.msichicago.org/whats-here/exhibits/farm-tech/
Visit the Farm Tech Exhibit to explore the latest technologies
farmers use, including robotic milking technology and using
manure for power.

# GLOSSARY

**allele**
An alternative form of a gene.

**asexual**
Lacking sex or functional sex organs (describing certain kinds of plants).

**bacterium**
A single-celled microorganism.

**biotechnology**
The manipulation of living organisms to produce useful products.

**DNA (deoxyribonucleic acid)**
A double helix consisting of complementary chains on which the genetic code is located.

**dominant**
A dominant gene allele is one that is expressed in preference to other alleles of that gene.

**ecosystem**
A localized group of interdependent organisms and the environment in which they live.

**genome**
The entire genetic material of an organism.

**hormone**
A chemical substance produced by an organism's body that exerts a regulatory or stimulatory effect.

**hybrid**
A plant produced from a cross between two plants that are of the same species but have different genetic constituents.

**insulin**
A hormone that regulates the level of glucose in the blood. Deficiency in production results in diabetes mellitus, an abnormal condition characterized by the secretion and excretion of excessive amounts of urine.

**monopoly**
>   A situation in which one company controls an industry or is the only provider of a product or service.

**organic**
>   Relating to agricultural practices that avoid using synthetic chemicals in favor of naturally occurring pesticides, fertilizers, and other growing aids.

**patent**
>   An exclusive right officially granted by a government to an inventor to make or sell an invention.

**recessive**
>   A recessive allele is not expressed when two different alleles of that gene are present. The trait controlled by the recessive allele only appears when two such alleles are present.

**species**
>   A basic biological classification that contains individuals that resemble one another and that may interbreed.

**strain**
>   A group of descendants from a common ancestor.

**synthesis**
>   The process of forming a complex compound combining simpler substances.

**vaccine**
>   A preparation containing weakened or dead microbes that cause a particular disease that is administered to stimulate the immune system to produce antibodies against that disease.

**virus**
>   A particle consisting of a core of DNA (deoxyribonucleic acid) or RNA (ribonucleic acid) that is surrounded by a protein coat. A virus cannot reproduce on its own, but it can infect a cell and take over the cell's molecular machinery.

# SOURCE NOTES

**Chapter 1. Breakthroughs in Biology**
None.

**Chapter 2. Organic Food**
1. Lester R. Brown, et al. *State of the World 1999: Millennium Edition*. New York: W.W. Norton/Worldwatch Institute, 1999. 169–170.
2. George Kuepper and Lance Gegner. "Organic Crop Overview: Fundamentals of Sustainable Agriculture." *National Sustainable Agriculture Information Service Online*. Aug. 2004. National Center for Appropriate Technology. 13 July 2008 <http://attra.ncat.org/attra-pub/organiccrop.html>.

**Chapter 3. Politics and Food**
1. Jennifer Kahn. "The Green Machine: Monsanto Co's Transgenic Products Tightens Their Control of Seed Market." *Harper's Magazine*. 1 Apr. 1999. Mindfully.org. 4 Aug. 2008. <http://www.mindfully.org/GE/Monsanto--Seed-Market1apr99.htm>.
2. Ibid.
3. Edgar J. DaSilva. "GMOs and Development." *Electronic Journal of Biotechnology*. 2002. 14 July 2008 <http://www.ejbiotechnology.info/content/issues/01/index.html>.

**Chapter 4. Benefits**
1. Gregory E. Pence. *Designer Food: Mutant Harvest or Bread Basket of the World?* New York: Rowman & Littlefield Publishers, Inc., 2002. 164.
2. Ibid. 34–35.

**Chapter 5. Risk and Expense**
1. Peter Pringle. *Food, Inc.: Mendel to Monsanto—The Promises and Perils of the Biotech Harvest*. New York: Simon & Schuster, 2003. 51.
2. Martin Teitel and Kimberly A. Wilson. *Genetically Engineered Food: Changing the Nature of Nature*. Rochester, VT: Park Street Press, 2001. 16.
3. Ibid. 18–19.

**Chapter 6. Testing**
1. "Statement of John Fagan/Suit Against FDA 28may99." *Mindfully. org.* 28 May 1999. 4 Aug. 2008
<http://www.mindfully.org/GE/Fagan-FDA-Suit-28may99.htm>.
2. "GM Foods and Denial of Rights and Choices: Interview with Arpad Pusztai." *Frontline* (India). 10 Nov. 2000. Transcript. Canadian Health Coalition. 14 July 2008
<http://www.healthcoalition.ca/pusztai.html>.
3. Daniel Charles. *Lords of the Harvest: Biotech, Big Money, and the Future of Food.* Cambridge, MA: Perseus Publishing, 2001. 137.
4. Marion Nestle. *Safe Food: Bacteria, Biotechnology, and Bioterrorism.* Berkeley, CA: University of California Press, 2003. 166.

**Chapter 7. Business Practices**
1. Gregory E. Pence. *Designer Food: Mutant Harvest or Breadbasket of the World?* New York: Rowman & Littlefield Publishers, Inc., 2002. 21.
2. Teresa Riordan. "Grace Unit's European Biotech Patent on Soybeans Meets Opposition." *New York Times* 1 Dec. 1994. 4 Aug. 2008 <http://query.nytimes.com/gst/
fullpage.html?res=9C03E2D81130F932A35751C1A962958260>.
3. Marion Nestle. *Safe Food: Bacteria, Biotechnology, and Bioterrorism.* Berkeley, CA: University of California Press, 2003. 227.
4. Martin Teitel and Kimberly A. Wilson. *Genetically Engineered Food: Changing the Nature of Nature.* Rochester, VT: Park Street Press, 2001.

**Chapter 8. Culture, Religion, and Humanity**
1. Martin Teitel and Kimberly A. Wilson. *Genetically Engineered Food: Changing the Nature of Nature.* Rochester, VT: Park Street Press, 2001. 96–97.
2. Peter Pringle. *Food, Inc.: Mendel to Monsanto—The Promise and Perils of the Biotech Harvest.* New York: Simon & Schuster, 2003. 86.
3. Greg Ciola. "Does Genetic Engineering Have God's Endorsement?" *Newswithviews.com.* 28 Mar. 2007. 11 July 2008
<http://www.newswithviews.com/Ciola/greg4.htm>.
4. "An HSUS Report: Welfare Issues with Genetic Engineering and Cloning of Farm Animals." *The Humane Society of the United States.* 29 Apr. 2008. 14 July 2008 <http://www.hsus.org/farm/resources/
research/practices/genetic_engineering_and_cloning_farm_animals.html>.

SOURCE NOTES CONTINUED

**Chapter 9. The Future of Genetic Engineering**
1. "About us." *Grain.org*. 24 July 2008. 4 Aug. 2008
<http://grain.org/about/>.
2. "ISAAA in Asia: Promoting corporate profits in the name
of the poor." Grain.org. 4 Aug. 2008. http://grain.org/
briefings/?id=137.
3. Ibid.
4. "ISAAA Brief 37_2007: Executive Summary: Global Status of
Commercialized Biotech/Gm Crops: 2007." *International Service for
the Acquisition of Agri-Biotech Applications*. 2007. 14 July 2008
<http://www.isaaa.org/resources/publications/briefs/37/
executivesummary/default.html>.
5. Marion Nestle. *Safe Food: Bacteria, Biotechnology, and Bioterrorism*.
Berkeley, CA: University of California Press, 2003. 141.

# INDEX

# INDEX NOTES CONTINUED

## ABOUT THE AUTHOR

Lillian E. Forman is a former high school teacher of English who now writes and edits educational materials for students. Forman has written about such diverse subjects as animals with jobs, kudzu, outer-space travel, the life of Coretta Scott King, and the interior of Earth. Forman also has published short stories for children. For her own pleasure, she writes personal essays and poetry.

## PHOTO CREDITS

AP Images, cover; Bettmann/Corbis, 6; Ben Greer/iStock Photo, 8; Charles Bennett/AP Images, 15; Ashley Cooper/Corbis, 16; Phototake/AP Images, 22; Erik Freeland/Corbis, 25; James A. Finley/AP Images, 26; Martin Cleaver/AP Images, 31; Dan Gill/AP Images, 35, 70; Micheline Pelletier/Sygma/Corbis, 36; Enrique Macarian/Reuters/Corbis, 39; Andreas Reh/iStock Photo, 45; Gustavo Graff/handout/epa/Corbis, 46; Mike Fiala/AP Images, 50; Daniel Maurer/AP Images, 55; iStock Photo, 56; Jim Richardson/Corbis, 60, 65; Elise Amendola/AP Images, 66; Jonathan Hayward/AP Images, 75; Luca Tettoni/Corbis, 76; Aaron Harris/AP Images, 80; Karel Navarro/AP Images, 85; Sakchai Lalit/AP Images, 86; Paul Sakuma/AP Images, 89; Frank van Haalen/iStock Photo, 95